MINISTRY OF MUNITIONS.

Technical Department—Aircraft Production.

CENTRAL HOUSE,
KINGSWAY, W.C.2.

I.C. 651.

TREND OF GERMAN AEROPLANE DESIGN.

NOVEMBER, 1918.

J. G. WEIR,
Brigadier-General,
Controller, Technical Department.

AIR MINISTRY.

Directorate of Research.

CENTRAL HOUSE,
KINGSWAY, W.C. 2,
June, 1919.

I.C. 665.

REPORT
by
Technical Commission on German Aeroplanes and Engines.

This report was made by representatives of the Directorate of Research, who proceeded to Fienvillers on January 23rd, 1919, and is circulated as being of interest until the more detailed reports are issued.

H. R. BROOKE-POPHAM,
Brigadier-General,
Director of Research.

The Naval & Military Press Ltd

Published by
The Naval & Military Press Ltd
5 Riverside, Brambleside, Bellbrook
Industrial Estate, Uckfield, East Sussex,
TN22 1QQ England

Tel: +44 (0) 1825 749494
Fax: +44 (0) 1825 765701

www.naval-military-press.com
www.military-genealogy.com

In reprinting in facsimile from the original, any imperfections are inevitably reproduced and the quality may fall short of modern type and cartographic standards.

MINISTRY OF MUNITIONS.

Technical Department—Aircraft Production.

CENTRAL HOUSE,
KINGSWAY, W.C.2.

I.G. 651.

TREND OF GERMAN AEROPLANE DESIGN.

NOVEMBER, 1918.

J. G. WEIR,
Brigadier-General,
Controller, Technical Department.

MINISTRY OF MUNITIONS.

Technical Department. — Aircraft Production.

Central House,

Kingsway, W.C.2.

I.C. 651.

Trend of German Aeroplane Design.

PERFORMANCE.

Enemy aeroplanes which have been captured intact or reconstructed have, under test, generally shown themselves poor in performance, judged by British standards, especially in point of speed at heights; but it would seem that as a rule they are fairly good in point of climb, and notably good in regard to manœuvrability. Pilots report them, in the main, comfortable to fly and easy to land, especially the more modern types.

WING SECTION.

Scale drawings showing the wing sections employed are included in the detailed reports on the various enemy aeroplanes. In general they do not differ very markedly from British wing sections, though there is a distinct tendency towards rather greater camber. It is thought probable that this principle has been adopted so as to yield better results at high altitudes when the angle of incidence would necessarily be somewhat big.

Practically all German aeroplanes have a pronounced wash-out at the tip of the trailing edge. In the most recent example of Halberstadt design, namely, the C4 type, the lower wings are given a heavy wash-out at their junction with the bottom of the fuselage, the idea being to minimise the surface of discontinuity which would otherwise exist between the bottom surface of the fuselage and the wing roots. Thus the front spar is straight, but the rear edge is markedly concave. This effect exists to such an extent that the trailing spar is considerably bent as well as twisted.

The Fokker wing section is in a class by itself, not only on account of its great depth, but also in having only a very slight camber on the bottom surface. The performance of this machine is, however, by no means despicable, and it is generally conceded to be a redoubtable opponent in spite of the departure from optimum wing section which has been made.

BAYS.

As far as single and two-seater machines are concerned, the usual wing construction involves a single pair of struts at each side, but it is noticeable that in the latest model Pfalz scout, the D12, this practice has given place to double pairs of struts. Indications point to great strength having been made a matter of prime importance in this design.

In some types, notably the Pfalz and the Fokker, the upper plane is made as a single unit. In the latter case, the lower plane is also in one piece. In the generality of machines, however, the centre section principle appears to be gaining vogue. Thus, whereas the L.V.G. C5 has a cabane consisting of the usual pyramid of struts, its successor, the C6, is furnished with a centre section embracing a gravity petrol tank and the radiator, both of which are let into the plane flush with its top and bottom surfaces. The Halberstadt and Hannoveraner designs employ the same scheme.

SPARS.

Shortage of ash and spruce has led to the general adoption of built-up spars, which are of such a variety of types that a separate report is being issued upon their design. In nearly all cases ply-wood plays an important part. Thus in the Fokker biplane the spar, which, owing to the absence of the usual wire bracing of the wings, is extremely deep, consists of two thin rails of spruce united by deep ply-wood webs. In the Gotha bomber a built up I section spruce spar is covered in with ply-wood at each side. On the Giant Four and Five-Engined bombers the spars are of hollow rectangular section, strengthened by a transverse web across the middle of the box. The latter is built of numerous components tongued and grooved together. The whole is strengthened by walls of multi-ply glued on each side. In the Halberstadt design the built-up spruce spars are reinforced by broad horizontal webs of ply-wood running longitudinally, and at each edge of these are stringers. The whole spar construction thus represents a section similar to an H lying on its side, of which the central box spar forms the cross bar.

The A.E.G. machines are alone in employing steel tubular spars.

Other German designs, such as the Pfalz, D.F.W., L.V.G., Rumpler, and Albatros employ built-up spars of the ordinary accepted type, either of box or I section.

WIRING.

With the exception of the Fokker biplane and triplane, which have no external wire bracing whatever in the wings, the rigging of German machines is upon the accepted lines. The standard material is multi-strand cable furnished with whipped and sweated splices at the loops. Quick detachment devices, which at one time were fitted on several German models, have now disappeared. For internal wiring, both plain wire and stranded cable are used. In the Fokker design, the angle of the drag bracing cables between the struts seems to be very bad, but according to reports this machine is actually unusually strong. Drag bracings are in some cases taken from the front of the fuselage, but in most designs are confined to the interior of the wings. In no case is the undercarriage used to form a component of the bracing system.

In most machines the compression struts between the spars, for drag bracing, are steel tubes, but in some cases, notably the Fokker, Halberstadt, and Albatros, wooden box ribs are used for this purpose.

FUSELAGES.

The standard type of German fuselage construction embodies a three-ply shell built up on light wooden formers. It is generally of the wireless form, but in some cases the forward portion in the neighbourhood of the wings and engine is strengthened with diagonal bracing. This is adopted also in the Gotha in that part of the body which embraces the cockpits and petrol tanks.

Exceptions from this general rule are the A.E.G. two-seater, the A.E.G. bomber, and the Fokker (biplane and triplane). In all of these steel is exclusively used for the fuselage construction, the transverse members being welded to the longerons. In the Four and Five-Engined Giant bombers the rear portion of the fuselage, including the longerons, is of steel tube, whilst in the Friedrichshafen bomber wooden longerons are used in conjunction with steel tube compression members.

In nearly all cases the wooden fuselage is roughly rectangular in section, with corners rounded off, and tapers to a vertical knife-edge at the rear. In the Halberstadt, on the contrary, it tapers, in a manner similar to that of the Bristol Fighter, to a horizontal edge. In the Pfalz designs great pains have been taken to produce a fish-shaped body of perfect streamline form; this is of approximately elliptical section throughout, though leaning towards a sharp " backbone " near the tail. The performance of this design is, however, relatively poor, and the rather elaborate streamlining appears to bring no great material benefits.

In the Albatros and the earlier Pfalz the fin is built in one with the fuselage, and very neatly faired off; but it is notable that in the latest Pfalz this practice has been discarded in favour of a detachable fin.

TAIL SURFACES.

The use of fixed fins and tail planes is now standard on all German aeroplanes, and in nearly all cases both the rudder and elevator are balanced. In some cases—notably the Fokker biplane—the fin is offset so as to mitigate the turning effect due to the swirl of the slipstream. In the Hannoveraner fighter a biplane tail is incorporated with a view to reducing the blind area of the movable machine gun.

In all the big bombers—the Gotha, the Friedrichshafen, and the Giant machines of both types—a biplane tail is now a standard fitting, though it has not yet been adopted on the A.E.G.

In practically all cases the framework of the tail organs is of light steel tube, and in general this applies to the fixed planes as well as to the controllable surfaces. In the Pfalz, Albatros, and L.V.G. designs the fixed plane frames are of wood, and covered with thin ply-wood.

In some cases—notably the A.E.G. bomber—the fixed planes are of heavily cambered streamline section. The same practice, though to a less noticeable extent, is embodied in the latest Halberstadt; but in the Fokker, which is to be regarded as one of the most up-to-date German types, flat uncambered surfaces are exclusively employed. In this case, too, the fixed tail plane is made in one unit and dropped into brackets on the top side of the fuselage, instead of being constructed in two halves, and placed one on either side. This principle has also been adopted in the most recent Halberstadt.

CONTROLS.

The control gear on German aeroplanes calls for very little comment, being, in all but the large bombers, of the standard universally jointed stick pattern. The arrangement of the rocking shaft varies, being, in some cases, fore and aft, and in others transverse. The rudder bars are almost invariably made of welded sheet steel, and are generally fitted with toe-straps. In recent machines the pilot's seat is frequently adjustable, whereas in earlier designs it was more common to find the leg reach adjustable on the rudder bar. In several cases a locking device is employed, so that the elevator can be fixed at any angle. In the Fokker biplane the control gear is extremely light compared with that of other enemy designs.

Wheel control for the ailerons is only used on the large bombers such as A.E.G., Gotha, and Friedrichshafen. In the first-named, a dual control for the elevator and rudder is provided, but in the others no form of dual control at all is found. In the Giant aeroplanes double control, operated by two pilots simultaneously, is adopted, as the physical effort called for is beyond the capacity of a single man.

STRUTS.

Probably owing to a shortage of timber, wooden interplane struts are very little used, and are only found in the Friedrichshafen, L.V.G., and the older type of Pfalz. Steel struts are either tubes of round section faired off with a three-ply or solid wood streamlining, or of oval section, the latter practice being increasingly popular. In some cases the strut ends are tapered and welded to a socket; in others the tube is kept full section, and is dropped over an eyebolt at each end. N struts for the junction of the top plane and the fuselage are common, and are also used between the planes in the Pfalz and Fokker models. Oval steel tubes for undercarriage struts are practically universal, the L.V.G. being the only design incorporating wooden members in this position.

FABRIC AND DOPE.

In general, there are two types of fabric found on enemy aeroplanes. They are of similar material, but differ in colouring. That intended for scouts and fighters is camouflaged in the familiar pattern of irregular polygons of light colours, whilst that for bombers is of such dark tones that the shapes of the polygons can scarcely be discerned. In some examples of the Fokker biplane the upper surface of the wings is painted a bright colour, such as red, over the top of the dyed camouflage scheme. The Pfalz was formerly covered with an aluminium dope, but this has now given way to the standard colouring.

The quality of fabric is, in general, good, but in most cases the dope seems to be carelessly applied, and not thoroughly "worked in" to the material, from which it readily peels off.

The bodies of aeroplanes are sometimes left natural wood colour, as in the L.V.G.; sometimes, as in the Fokker, painted in two bands of bright colours; but more often covered with a cloudy camouflage effect, consisting of soft, low-toned colours, gradually fading into one another and apparently sprayed on.

PILOT'S VIEW.

It would appear that in recent designs the necessity of giving the pilot a good view has received more consideration than in the past. The Fokker, Hannoveraner, and Halberstadt machines are excellent in this respect. The bombers seem also to be good, with the exception of the A.E.G., which is very awkward indeed.

UNDERCARRIAGE.

For scouts and two-seaters the plain axle slung to V struts is invariably adopted. In most cases neither the axle nor the tie rod are faired off, but in the Fokker types, both monoplane and triplane, the axle fairing has been developed into a lifting surface. In the larger bombing machines current practice varies considerably. Thus in the Friedrichshafen there are three two-wheeled axles—one under each engine and the third under the nose of the fuselage. This system has been adopted in some of the Giant aeroplanes. In the Gotha there are two two-wheeled axles under each engine, whilst in the four-engined Giant under each engine unit is a ponderous single axle supporting at each end four wheels placed side by side.

SHOCK ABSORBERS.

Rubber bands have now entirely disappeared, and their place has been taken by steel coil springs. In some cases three coils, of alternate "hand," are placed one inside the other; in others, three small coils are grouped together in a "clover leaf" and covered in with cotton fabric. The weight of spring used on the average machine is about 5 lbs. for each wheel. In the Gotha the shock-absorber springs are concealed in the undercarriage struts, and are worked by a cable passing over pulleys. Steel-shod wooden tail skids are almost always used, but are not made steerable.

ENGINE BEARERS.

In most scouts and two-seaters wooden bearers, sometimes of ash, but more often of pine, are supported on multi-ply-wood bulkheads, but in the Fokker and A.E.G. designs the construction is of steel tubes, to which flat clips are fixed for the support of the crankcase arms. In the A.E.G. bomber the bearers are hollow steel of rectangular section. Owing to shortage of suitable timber, the bearers on the Giant aeroplanes, which are necessarily very long, are built up of a soft wood centre piece, reinforced top and bottom with five half-inch layers of ash.

ENGINE CONTROLS.

On a few machines—notably the Hannoveraner—this is fitted in duplicate, there being, in addition to the usual throttle lever, another controlled by Bowden wire from the control stick. In the multiple-engined bombers separate engine throttle levers for each engine are installed, and in the two-engine type they are so placed as to be operated together when required. The same applies to ignition advance levers, but where Mercedes engines are used the ignition control is coupled up to the throttle.

RADIATORS.

Several types of radiators are in use on German aeroplanes, and in nearly all cases they are fitted with some simple form of shutter, which is used in conjunction with an electrical rheostat thermometer. Formerly it was the general practice, especially in two-seaters of the D.F.W., Rumpler, A.E.G., and L.V.G. patterns to mount a rectangular radiator in front of the cabane, just underneath the top plane; but in the latest L.V.G.s this method has been discarded, and a curved radiator sunk flush in the centre section is adopted in its place. Generally speaking, this plane radiator is now standard in two-seater designs, but in the Pfalz, which previously incorporated this scheme, the latest pattern has a nose radiator of vertical tubes, the arrangement being somewhat similar to that of the Fokker biplane; these two machines are in this respect in a class by themselves.

On bombers the usual design embraces a car type radiator at the front end of the engine bearers, but in the four and five-engine Giant machines the use of gear boxes has prevented this practice being adhered to, and in these the radiators are carried well up above the motors, and fixed either on the engine bearer struts or on wires.

In the flush pattern of radiator the tubes are horizontal and of flattened oval section, and are set with their major axis inclined. The tubes are in two cells, which are separated by baffle plates, which ensure that the water runs from side to side, then down, and then from side to side back again. A short-circuit tube is nearly always provided to guard against the formation of air locks in the upper portion of the water tank. Another fitting frequently met with is a small subsidiary water tank mounted above the radiator and connected to the main filler cap with a tube. The top of this tank is fitted with a trumpet-shaped nozzle pointing forward.

GEARS.

It is significant that in the four and five-engined Giant aeroplanes massive gear boxes are used in conjunction with standard engines of the Mercedes and Maybach type. As might be expected with six-cylinder motors, the gear boxes are very heavy. In the four-engine machines they had shallow casings fitted with cast aluminium cooling fins, and were connected to the engines by flexible couplings and external shafts. In the five-engine design the shafts are enclosed within the gear box. Plain spur pinions are fitted, and the ratio employed both for tractor and pusher screws is 21/41. The gear boxes are of two distinct types—a short one for the tractor screw and a long one for the pusher. The latter is given considerable overhang in order to obviate the need for cutting away a section of the trailing edge to give clearance for the screw. This idea had been adopted both on the Friedrichshafen and Gotha designs, doubtless with some noticeable loss in efficiency.

Each gear box, including the flywheel on the engine which it necessitates, the flexible coupling, and the oil radiator, adds a weight of 346 lbs.—a little over 1.15 lb. per H.P. It is obvious, however, that the gain in propulsive efficiency is considerable.

The oil radiator referred to consists of a semi-circular tank slung under the gear box, and containing 65 tubes of, roughly, 20 mm. diameter. Oil is circulated through this and the sump in the gear box by a pinion pump driven through worm gears and a flexible shaft from the driving pinion shaft of the gear box.

PETROL SYSTEMS.

These generally incorporate two tanks—one gravity and one under pressure supplied by an engine pump—except where Benz engines are installed. In this case a petrol pump is employed, which supplies a tubular chamber, from which the overflow returns to the main tank: a hand petrol pump of the semi-rotary type is used for filling the gravity starting tank. The last-named is frequently let flush into the centre section of the upper plane, or is strapped on to it, except in the D.F.W. and Pfalz designs. In the former it is placed on the top of the main tank, and forms the back of the pilot's seat; in the latter it is under the engine cowling. In the Fokker, the main, auxiliary, and oil tanks are incorporated in one unit, and a hand pressure pump is fitted for starting purposes. A small windmill, similar to that on the D.H.9 aeroplane, was found in the wreckage of the five-engined Giant, and it is conjectured that the enemy may have turned his attention to this kind of petrol supply mechanism.

PROPELLERS.

Owing to the shortage of the best classes of timber, mahogany and walnut are now frequently replaced by ash, pine, sycamore, and maple. The screws of the Giant bombers, being geared down, roughly, 2 to 1, are not very heavily stressed, and are made entirely of soft wood covered with thin veneer, the grain of which runs across the blade.

WIRELESS.

The majority of German aeroplanes are internally wired for greater wireless capacity, but are only fitted with transmitting apparatus when this is actually going to be used. In some cases the dynamo is driven from a pulley on the engine in conjunction with a hand-controlled clutch, but in modern types it is commoner to find the dynamo supported on one of the undercarriage struts, and driven by a screw in the slip-stream of the tractor. On the five-engined Giant a Douglas type horizontally opposed engine of about 3 H.P. drives the wireless and heating generator.

ARMAMENT.

On scouts it is now usual to find two fixed guns firing through the screw and furnished with the usual interrupter gear operated by Bowden wire from the pilot's control stick. On some two-seater machines provision has been made for two fixed guns, but generally only one is fitted. The mountings for the movable observer's gun vary considerably, but in most machines they comprise wooden rings of rather clumsy design. In the Halberstadt it is notable that the gun mounting is erected well above the top of the fuselage, and is streamlined in section as much as possible.

The chief machine designed for offensives against troops in trenches is the armoured A.E.G. two-seater. In this case the pilot has no gun at all, but the observer has three— one movable on a rotating turret, and two fixed weapons firing forward and downward, at an angle of 45 deg. through the floor. It appears that the only other armoured aeroplanes are the Junker and the Albatross, but examples of this type have not been captured.

BOMBS.

Small bombs are invariably carried in vertical magazine racks inside the fuselage, and discharged through a trap-door in the floor. The larger bombs are fitted in cradles under the fuselage, and also underneath the wing roots. On the later Gothas an electrical signal device is used to indicate that the bomb has actually left the machine. On these machines the medium-sized bombs appear to be generally released in pairs.

W.G.A., Ap.D. (L.),

J. G. WEIR,
Brigadier-General,
Controller, Technical Department.

AIR MINISTRY.

Directorate of Research.

I.C. 665.

CENTRAL HOUSE,
KINGSWAY, W.C. 2,
June, 1919.

REPORT

by

Technical Commission on German Aeroplanes and Engines.

This report was made by representatives of the Directorate of Research, who proceeded to Fienvillers on January 23rd, 1919, and is circulated as being of interest until the more detailed reports are issued.

H. R. BROOKE-POPHAM,
Brigadier-General,
Director of Research.

Report by Technical Commission on German Aeroplanes and Engines.

THE THREE SECTIONS OF THIS REPORT ARE CONCERNED RESPECTIVELY WITH—
1, AEROPLANES; 2, ENGINES; 3, ARMAMENT.

SECTION I (AEROPLANES.)

The following notes anticipate the detailed and fully illustrated reports, which will be issued when the various machines arrive in England.

Among the aeroplanes inspected were several new designs which have not yet been in service, and one or two of the older standard types modified.

NEW TYPES OF AEROPLANES.

1. **Two-Seater Gotha Fighter.**—This is an exceedingly interesting machine and is in general modelled on the lines of the D.H. 10; it is, however, apparently intended for fighting rather than bombing purposes, as no bomb racks were found on these machines.

The aeroplane is of the tractor type, driven by two 260 H.P. Mercedes engines. These are contained in very smoothly faired eggs, built up of 3-ply wood and detachable metal cowlings, which rest upon the centre section of the lower planes. (See photograph.) The latter is also covered top and bottom with ply wood, whilst the wing extensions are in all cases covered with fabric.

FUSILAGE AND TAIL UNIT OF TWIN-ENGINED TWO-SEATER GOTHA FIGHTER.

ENGINE INSTALLATION IN TWO-SEATER GOTHA FIGHTER.

The fuselage is built up of ply wood on the usual wooden longerons. The forward part of the fuselage is permanently fixed to the centre section and engine unit, and the rearward part is built to it, the joint being at an angle to the axis of the fuselage.

The engine eggs are braced to the forward portion of the body by composite steel and ply wood struts. They are not attached in any way to the upper plane.

The nose of the fuselage is covered with a round fairing of beaten metal and the general appearance of the machine is very pleasing to the eye.

It is evident that great care has been taken to reduce its resistance as far as possible. This is shown in the arrangements of the water pipes connecting the engine to the flat radiators, which are let into the top planes immediately over the motors. The water pipes are of a triangular section and are placed base to base.

The centre section of the lower plane has square ends and the wings are attached by the usual pin joints. The upper wings are carried by a top centre section, which is triangular in form with the apex pointed forward.

This top centre section contains two gravity petrol tanks.

The honeycomb radiators have inclined tubes and over the top of each is a shutter, the front edge of which is hinged whilst the rear edge can be opened or closed by means of rods and levers fitted on the trailing edge of the triangular centre section.

The upper plane centre section is braced to the fuselage by means of streamline steel tubular struts.

Accommodation is provided for one pilot and one observer. Lateral control is by wheel; no form of dual control is provided. The observer's cockpit carries a gun mounting of wood of the imitation Scarff type.

A second gun can be mounted so as to fire through the rearward fuselage tunnel, which extends nearly to the tail of the machine.

The observer sits on a small hammock type of seat, and has foot rests, one on each side of the fuselage.

His position cannot be described as particularly comfortable, but both he and the pilot have a good field of vision.

The main petrol tank is under the pilot's seat, but is not of large enough capacity for this machine to make very long flights.

The oil tanks are inside the engine eggs and are fitted with glass levels visible from the pilot's seat.

The revolution counters are also mounted on the eggs.

Balanced ailerons are fitted, and a feature of these is the fact that the balance vane is separated from the aileron plane proper by a slot about 4 in. wide. It is not obvious why this arrangement has been adopted.

TAIL PLANE UNIT OF TWIN-ENGINED TWO-SEATER GOTHA FIGHTER.

The tail design is reminiscent of the biplane arrangement on the Gotha bombers. It is shallow in gap and furnished with two elevators and two rudders. The lower elvator is of 3-ply and the upper of fabric.

The fixed fin and tail planes are both covered with 3-ply, and the former is faired off into the upper surface of the fuselage.

The tail skid is of the laminated spring type. The propellers have a diameter of 3·05 metres and a pitch of 2·05 metres. They are provided with large spinners forming smooth nose pieces to the engine eggs.

The pilot is furnished with a fixed Spandau gun firing dead ahead through the space between the screw discs.

The weights of the Gotha 2-seater as inscribed on the fuselage are as follows :—

Weight, empty	2,514 kg.
Useful weight	720 kg.
Total weight	3,234 kg.

It is hoped that performance tests on this interesting machine will be carried out at an early date.

2. **A.E.G. Armoured Bomber.**—This machine embraces so many modifications from the previous A.E.G. Twin engine bomber that it may fairly be described as a new type, although the general arrangement of the planes, etc., is very similar to the previous one.

A.E.G. TWIN-ENGINED ARMOURED BOMBER.
(Front view shewing mounting for heavy calibre gun.)

The construction is of steel throughout, with the exception of the ribs of the main planes, which are of wood threaded on to steel tube spars.

The engines are 260 H.P. Mercedes, driving tractor screws, and are mounted in metal-panelled eggs supported by steel struts from the upper to the lower planes, and also heavily strutted to the fuselage. The latter is much narrower than formerly, and provides accommodation for a crew of three, one pilot, one forward gunner and one after gunner. No dual control is fitted.

The principal feature of the machine is the armour plating, which covers the sides and base of the fuselage, and extends from the nose to the rear of the after gunner's cockpit, behind which a V-shaped panel of plating is fixed.

The under-sides of the engine eggs are also armour plated.

The forward gunner is armed with a Parabellum gun, mounted on an imitation Scarff ring. On the floor and arranged to fire horizontally forward through an arc of about 60 deg. is a mounting for a gun—presumed to be about 1½ pounder. This is fixed to a rotatable mounting, which is protected by a semi-circular shield of armour plate, which moves with the gun, as also does the gunner's seat.

A.E.G. ARMOURED BOMBER.

Inside front of gunner's cockpit (shewing mounting for heavy calibre gun).

A second Scarff mounting with Parabellum gun is provided for the after gunner, who manages a 1½ pounder, fixed to fire downwards through a trap-door in the floor ; at all events this is assumed to be the case by the disposition and size of the fittings.

The weight of this machine being much greater than that of the original A.E.G. bomber and the power plant the same, it is presumed that its speed capacities are lower, but its armament would make it a formidable antagonist and it was evidently principally designed for " ground strafing " purposes.

This machine is fitted with a rearward fuselage tunnel, through which the movable after machine gun can be fired downwards and backwards. The base of the tunnel is covered in with a detachable panel of fabric.

No inter-communication is possible between the three cockpits, nor are any small bomb magazines carried.

Under the sections of the lower main plane, immediately below the engine eggs, are four racks for bombs of about 50 kg. weight.

An interesting point is that for purposes of easy transport the engine sections, together with the undercarriages, are fixed in a light steel framing fitted with a castor wheel, and a long draw bar. Temporary undercarriages are in like manner fitted to the fuselage.

Three vertical tubes about 2 feet long and provided with a release mechanism are fitted into the floor of the after gunner's cockpit, and four tubes of a similar type on the forward cockpit. These are assumed to be for purposes of signal lights, but it is possible that they serve some other object as they are different from any previously seen in other German machines.

3. **Albatros C.I.B.**—This is a wooden construction 2-seater reconnaissance machine, closely following in general lines the design of the L.V.G. C.5. It has a square section fuselage covered in with 3-ply, and the upper main planes are supported by means of detachable bolts to a tubular steel cabane formed of A struts.

The engine is 180 H.P. Mercedes, and the only notable feature of the installation is the use of a radiator made in sections, each consisting of about 80 honeycomb cells bolted together. This radiator has a semi-circular projection in front, which contains adjustable slides so that the amount of air entering the radiator can be adjusted. When the blinds are quite or nearly closed, the whole is of approximate streamline section.

The control for the ailerons is by wheel, and the only point that is characteristically Albatros is the faired root of the 3-ply fin and the covering of the body.

The workmanship in this machine is comparatively poor.

The armament consisted of a fixed Spandau firing through the air screw, and a Parabellum mounted on an imitation Scarff mounting.

4. **Fokker Monoplane.**—This is a new design which should yield interesting results, when its performance can be investigated. In general, it follows very closely the lines of the D.7 biplane, from which it differs of course in having a single main plane arranged in the parasol fashion.

No external wiring of any kind is used and the spars of the plane are supported by two pairs of V struts on each side, which spring from the tubular longerons of the fuselage.

When examined the machine was not assembled, but the pilot's eyes are apparently on a level with the trailing edge.

An auxiliary plane surrounds the undercarriage axle and is of the usual Fokker construction; it is covered with 3-ply wood and is deep enough to allow the axle to move up and down.

The construction of the fuselage is identical in principle with that of the biplane except that in order to fair off the circular engine cowling light wooden framework are fixed at each side and also on the top to support the fabric.

The engine is the standard Oberursel Le Rhone, and the cowling covers about two-thirds of its disc.

The date on this machine is 7/9/18.

5. **Gotha Bomber.**—Only detail modifications exist in the latest types of this machine, and it appears that some trouble has been taken to get down the weight.

An arrangement is made whereby the personnel—four in number—can change places, a shallow ledge, along which they can crawl, being let into the petrol tanks at one side; the latter separate the pilot's seat from the rear gunner's cockpit.

German bombing machines are now fitted with a biplane tail, which has already been described.

Instead of the old type of metal gun mounting in the front cockpit, a wooden one of imitation Scarff pattern is now fitted, and a sector is cut out of the ring and the turret to enable the gunner to obtain access.

Immediately aft of the hole which is cut in the top side of the fuselage to allow the after gunner to fire through the tunnel, is a peculiar shaped hump which is carefully faired off. The object of this is not known. Presumably it is introduced in order to give a better streamline formation to the rear edge of this hole, which, of course, acts as an entering edge.

A feature of the machine is the fitting of a very small secondary flap to the trailing edge of each aileron. The flap is operated by a separate lever from that of the main aileron, with which, however, it is in some way coupled as no separate control is found. The object of this flap can only be conjectured.

No change is found in the power plant (260 H.P. Mercedes engine) and undercarriages (four wheels on each side).

It is noticed that the engine revolution counters are of the electrical type, though this particular accessory seems to be somewhat heavier than the original centrifugal device.

6. **Albatros Armoured Machine (Type J.2.).**—This machine is similar to the A.E.G. armoured aeroplane, except that a wooden construction is used instead of steel tubing.

The armour plating is built on a wooden frame, and performs no structural function.

On the front of the fuselage four plates arranged in the form of a truncated pyramid surround the propeller shaft, but this is the only attempt to fair off the machine, the armour being otherwise applied in large flat sheets, though there are two inclined plates arranged to protect the Scarff gun mounting in the after cockpit. This is rather broader than the fuselage, and would otherwise overhang.

To allow the pilot easy access to his seat large doors of armour plate are fitted at each side and furnished with massive bolts.

The body behind the armour plate is similar to that of the Halberstadt, the apex coming to a horizontal knife edge. It is covered in with 3-ply which, unlike that of most German aeroplanes, is very notably cockled, and may be presumed to have been made of unseasoned wood.

The machine is fitted with wheel control.

The radiator is carried in the top plane.

7. **Pfalz D.8.**—This is a single-seater scout differing most notably from the usual Pfalz type in being fitted with a rotary Siemens-Schuckert engine. The construction is otherwise on the same lines as the older Pfalz biplane in all respects and is of wood.

Very small fixed tail planes and very large elevators are fitted and in like manner the rudder is very large indeed compared to the fixed fin.

The root of the latter is smoothly faired into the fuselage but unlike former practice in Pfalz machine the tail planes are not similarly faired.

It was noted that the propeller is of unusually large diameter with very narrow blades. Presumably this machine was more or less a failure and was superseded by the D.12 type upon which a full report has already been made.

8. **Junker J.1.**—A preliminary report has already been issued on this type of armoured aeroplane, and the detailed report awaits the arrival of a complete fuselage in England.

JUNKER J.I. ALL METAL BIPLANE.

JUNKER J.I. ALL METAL.

SECTION 2.—(ENGINES).

Comparatively little description of the design of the engines used in the machines which have been handed over is necessary, as, with the exception of the new Siemens-Schuckert, each of the surrendered aeroplanes is fitted with an engine of standard type dealt with in the reports already issued by the Directorate of Research, or now in preparation.

With regard to the Siemens-Schuckert (a new type of rotary engine used in the Pfalz Scouts) only two engines of this type were obtained, one of which it is understood has already been sent to E.R.S. for examination and tests, and the other, which is incomplete, has been sent to England for report. The following is a list of all the various types of aeroplanes and their respective engines examined at Fienvillers.

LIST OF GERMAN AEROPLANES AND TYPES OF ENGINES USED.

Type of Machine.	Type of Engine fitted.
A.E.G. Armoured fighter	230 H.P. Benz.
A.E.G. bomber	Two 260 H.P. Mercedes.
Albatros armoured	230 H.P. H.C. Benz.
Albatros scout	180 H.P. Mercedes. or 200 H.P. H.C. Mercedes..
Albatros two-seater fighter. (C.I.B.)	230 H.P. H.C. Benz.
D.F.W.	230 H.P. Benz.
Fokker monoplane	110 H.P. Oberursel (Le Rhone).
Fokker D. V11	200 H.P. H.C. Mercedes. or 200 H.P. Bayern.
Gotha night bomber	Two 260 H.P. Mercedes.
Gotha fighter (new type)	Two 260 H.P. Mercedes.
Hannoveranner	180 H.P. Opel Argus.
Halberstadt fighter	180 H.P. Mercedes. or 200 H.P. H.C. Mercedes.
Junker-armoured trench fighter	230 H.P. H.C. Benz.
L.V.G.	160 H.P. Mercedes. or 180 H.P. Mercedes.
Pfalz scout	180 H.P. Mercedes. or Siemen Schukert.
Rumpler fighter	300 H.P. Maybach.

A brief description of the later types of engines used in the surrendered machines, together with reference report numbers of those engines already published is given below. The complete list of Enemy Aero Engines is as follows :—

1. 160 H.P. Mercedes.
2. 180 H.P. Mercedes.
3. 200 H.P. High Compression Mercedes.
4. 260 H.P. Mercedes.
5. 200 H.P. Bayern (aluminium pistons).
6. 230 H.P. Benz.
7. 230 H.P. High Compression Benz (aluminium pistons).
8. 300 H.P. Maybach.
9. 180 H.P. Opel-Argus (aluminium pistons).
10. 110 H.P. Oberursel (German Le Rhone).
11. 160 H.P. Siemens-Schuckert.

It should be noted that the following recent types of Enemy engines were not used in any of the machines examined :—

270 H.P. Basse-Selve.

200 H.P. Austro-Daimler.

230 H.P. Hiero (Austro Fiat).

1. **160 H.P. Mercedes.**—A few engines of this type were brought in fitted to the older type of L.V.G. Hannoveranner and Albatros machines. The engine is now well-known and requires no description.

2. **180 H.P. Mercedes.**—Bore 140 mm., stroke 160 mm. A full report is in existence on this engine, which is an improved model of the old 160 H.P. Mercedes, with slightly higher compression and incorporating some of the features of the 260 H.P. Mercedes.

3. **200 H.P. High Compression Mercedes.**—Bore 140 mm., stroke 160 mm.

This engine is similar to the 180 H.P. Mercedes, but embodies several modifications and improvements in design, being fitted with an automatic altitude compensator in the carburetter. This device prevents the conical air valve below the throttle from lifting until the engine is opened out. The compression ratio has been raised from 4·64 to 5·73 by fitting domed pistons, which are still of cast iron with steel crowns, in place of the standard concave pistons. A fully detailed report of this engine, including results of tests carried out at R.A.E. is now ready for issue.

4. **260 H.P. Mercedes.**—Bore 160 mm., stroke 180 mm., Several minor improvements have been introduced since a detailed report on the original and standard type of 260 H.P. Mercedes, H. 29, was issued. The new features are as follows:—

Induction Pipe.—In the earlier models, several of which are fitted in the newest Gotha machines, the induction pipes are lagged with asbestos cord. In the latest types the lower portion of the induction pipes is provided with a welded steel water jacket, and supplied by a branch pipe from the water pump main circulation pipe, and a thermocouple is now fitted in the top of the main water outlet pipes above the cylinders leading to the radiators. The thermocouple is, of course, connected to a gauge on the dashboard. Flame dampers are now provided on the standard exhaust manifold as shown in the photographs of the 260 H.P. Mercedes Gotha Installation units. These consist of perforated outer casings to the exhaust manifolds.

The construction of the tubular aluminium casing for the camshaft vertical driving-shaft has also been slightly altered, being of much smaller diameter. The complete installation of the 260 H.P. Mercedes engines in the separate units, which form the upper portion of each of the two four-wheeled landing chassis, is of interest. Two views of the complete unit ready for transport are shown in the photographs attached.

260 H.P. MERCEDES GOTHA INSTALLATION.
(Unit ready for transport.)

260 H.P. MERCEDES GOTHA INSTALLATION.
(Unit ready for transport.)

The design of the streamlined cowling of the 260 H.P. Mercedes engines used in the new type two-seater Gotha machines is extremely well carried out, and is shown in the photographs.

5. **200 H.P. Bayern.**—Bore 150 mm., stroke 180 mm.

These engines are fitted as an alternative to the 200 H.P. Mercedes in many of the large number of Fokker D. VII machines handed over. They are of the usual six cylinder vertical type, and closely resemble the 180 H.P. and 200 H.P. Mercedes engines.

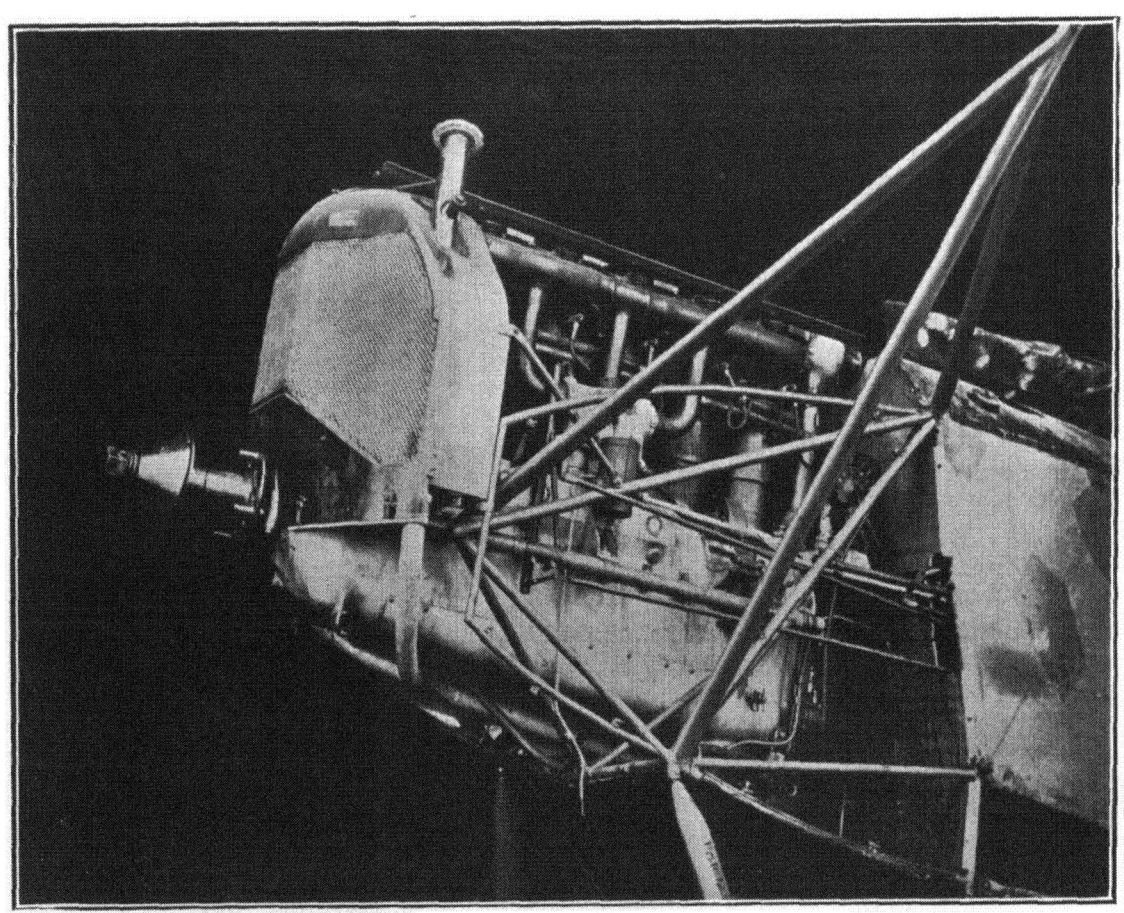

200 BAYERN ENGINE IN FOKKER D.7 BIPLANE.

The compression ratio is exceptionally high, being no less than 6·5 : 1.

The very close resemblance between the Bayern and the 180 H.P. Mercedes engines, illustrates how consistently the Germans have adhered to previous well tried designs. With the exception of the carburetter, which is entirely new, nearly all the features which depart from Mercedes practice have been adapted from other enemy engines, as, for example, the use of tubular type connecting rods and aluminium pistons.

The base-chamber is interesting, and compares favourably with that of the Mercedes, being better cooled and of lighter construction.

Provision is made for fitting the carburetter on either side of the engine ; it is thus possible by altering the timing of the engine and changing over the sparking plugs and carburetter, to bring the exhaust of the engine on either side as required.

The cylinders are, to a great extent, built on the same lines as those used in the 180 H.P. Mercedes, but are of greater capacity, and, as in the latter engine, are fitted with single inlet and exhaust valves.

Aluminium pistons are fitted. These are of excellent design and are heavily ribbed under the domed crowns.

The connecting rods are of tubular cross section and have only two big end bolts ; floating cast iron bushes are provided in the little end bearings.

The inlet and exhaust valves are operated by an overhead camshaft running in plain bronze bearings, and a half compression gear is fitted at the rear end.

The propeller thrust is taken by a single thrust ball race fitted at the front end, and an interesting type of propeller hub is fitted to the tapered extension of the crankshaft. A sectional view of this propeller hub is shown in the sketch. (Fig. I.)

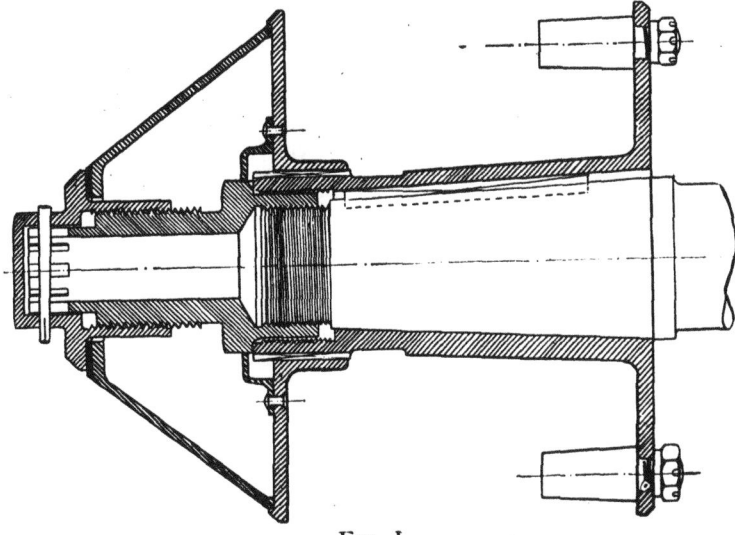

FIG. I.

The lubrication system generally follows Mercedes practice, but the method of feeding the camshaft from the front journal bearing is a new departure in enemy engines.

A centrifugal type water pump is fitted at the rear end of the crankcase and is driven directly off the bottom end of the vertical shaft which drives the oil pump. The two Bosch magnetos are driven transversely at the rear end of the engine. A bed is cast and machined on the induction side of the crankcase to take the wireless dynamo, which is driven by a train of gears off the vertical shaft. The machine gun interrupter gear is driven directly off the rear end of the crankshaft by flexible shafts.

Full particulars are given in a detailed report which will be issued shortly, the engine still being under test at R.A.E.

6. **230 H.P. Benz.**—Bore 145 mm., stroke 190 mm. Compression ratio, 4·95.

A complete detailed report on this engine has already been issued.

7. **230 H.P. High Compression Benz.**—Bore 145 mm., stroke 190 mm. Compression ratio, 5·82. Weight of complete engine dry, 855 lbs. = 3·75 lbs. per H.P.

Two test reports on this engine have been issued by R.A.E. and A.P.O., S.5., B.E.F.

The engine is similar in design to the standard 230 H.P. Benz, but is fitted with aluminium pistons and a modified design of oil pump and lubrication system. A separate report has also been published on the aluminium pistons.

8. **300 H.P. Maybach.**—Bore 165 mm., stroke 180 mm.

Full details and tests of this interesting engine as fitted to all the Rumpler machines are given in a report numbered H.B. 815.

9. **180 H.P. Opel-Argus.**—Bore 145 mm., stroke 160 mm. Compression ratio, 4·75 : 1.

A test report on this engine has already been issued by the R.A.E. (No. E. 1412), and a detailed report is in preparation.

10. **110 H.P. Oberursel.**—This engine, which is practically identical in design with the 110 H.P. French Le Rhone, with the exception of the aluminium pistons and the valve stems, has been fully dealt with in a comparative dimensional report No. HB. 814. Only one of these engines (fitted in a damaged Fokker Monoplane) was brought in.

11. **Siemens-Schuckert.**—No details of these new engines are at present available as the only engines delivered have been already sent to E.R.S. and to England (probably Islington). If possible it would be satisfactory if both these engines could be sent to R.A.E. for tests and investigation as soon as possible.

SECTION 3.—(ARMAMENT).

The most important points relating to each type of machine seen are mentioned below.

Junker Biplane, Type J. 1. Two-seater armoured trench fighter.—The observer is placed behind the pilot and has one Parabellum gun mounted on the ordinary rotating mounting, to be found on most German two-seaters, and also two Spandau guns, shooting through the floor of the cockpit, on the port side, of the machine, and pointing forward at an angle of 45 deg. The pilot is not provided with a forward firing gun. The ammunition for the Spandau guns is carried on rotating drums holding about 550 rounds per gun. These guns are not capable of movement in any direction. The front portion of the fuselage is heavily armoured to protect the engine pilot and observer.

Pfalz, Type D. XII. Single-seater fighter.—The armament of this machine consists of two Spandau guns, synchronised to fire through the propeller.

The synchronising gear used is of the usual German pattern, namely, a rotating flexible drive, which is thrown in and out of gear by a dog clutch operated by a Bowden cable, from the control lever of the machine. The guns are mounted on pressed up steel cradles, the latter being bolted to two cross members of the fuselage.

The front gun support is a fork which is capable of turning in a bearing, in the cradle itself, in a lateral plane ; the vertical and lateral adjustment are in the rear support fork, vertical adjustment is by screw and two nuts either side of a plate forming the base of the gun cradle ; lateral adjustment is provided by moving the rear support fork sideways. The bolts holding the fork to the cradle move in slots.

The ammunition boxes are not staggered and hold approximately 360 rounds per gun.

The empty cases are discharged overboard through a small chute which fits up against the discharge hole of the gun.

The empty belt passes through a chute (in the form of a large tube, on most machines and on others a built-up chute) into a receptacle in front of the ammunition box.

The control for the firing of the guns is on the top of the control lever on the machine ; it consists of a steel tube welded to the top of the control lever to form a T, with the arms of the T drooping downwards. To these are fitted celluloid bicycle grips ; the levers operating the guns are pivoted round the tube, forming the control lever of the machine, and to operate the guns they are pulled by the second and third finger towards the right hand arm of the handle described above.

Fokker Parasol Monoplane, Type E.V., Oberursel Le Rhone Engine.—Two forward firing Spandau guns. The synchronising gear is driven off the engine gear by a spur wheel which also drives the revolution counter.

The general arrangement of the armament of this machine is similar to the Pfalz, but the guns are not provided with adjustable mountings.

The only points of interest upon this machine are that both guns are provided with a rounds counter, which starts at 1,000 rounds and gives the number of rounds left, although the ammunition box only holds 650 rounds.

The counter is fitted to the rear of the gun, and is driven off a rod which is attached to the left hand side plate of the gun.

A good loading handle is fitted to the guns. This handle engages through gearing on the hubs of the crank handle of the gun ; a sample of this handle is being sent to the Directorate of Research for detailed inspection.

The gun control is fitted to the top of the control lever of the machine and incorporates a handle for working the throttle.

The empty belt is collected in a receptacle forward of the ammunition box, and the empty cases are discharged overboard.

A.E.G., Type J.2., Armoured two-seater trench fighter.—The armament of this machine consists of two Spandau guns in the observer's cockpit, behind the pilot, mounted in the same manner as in the Junker, and one Parabellum gun mounted on a rotating ring mounting.

L.V.G., Type, C. VI. Two-seater reconnaissance machine.—The armament of this machine consists of one Spandau synchronised in the usual German way for the pilot and one Parabellum on a ring mounting for the observer.

The Spandau is mounted on an adjustable mounting, but the forward gun support is not capable of turning in a horizontal plane as in the Pfalz; therefore, when the lateral adjustment is brought into use the front gun support must spring slightly.

The vertical adjustment is by three screws with nuts on either side of a plate, which is the horizontal face of a piece of angle iron. The lateral adjustment is effected by moving the angle iron sideways.

The bolts holding this plate to a ply-wood bulk-head in the fuselage move in slots in the vertical face of the angle iron.

The ammunition box holds about 1,000 rounds, and a receptacle is provided in front of the box to collect the empty belt; the ammunition box can be taken out to load it.

The empty cases pass through a small pipe and are discharged overboard.

The Parabellum gun is fitted with a special mounting to give a universal swivelling effect and to carry the drum for the ammunition. A sample of the mounting is being forwarded for detailed examination.

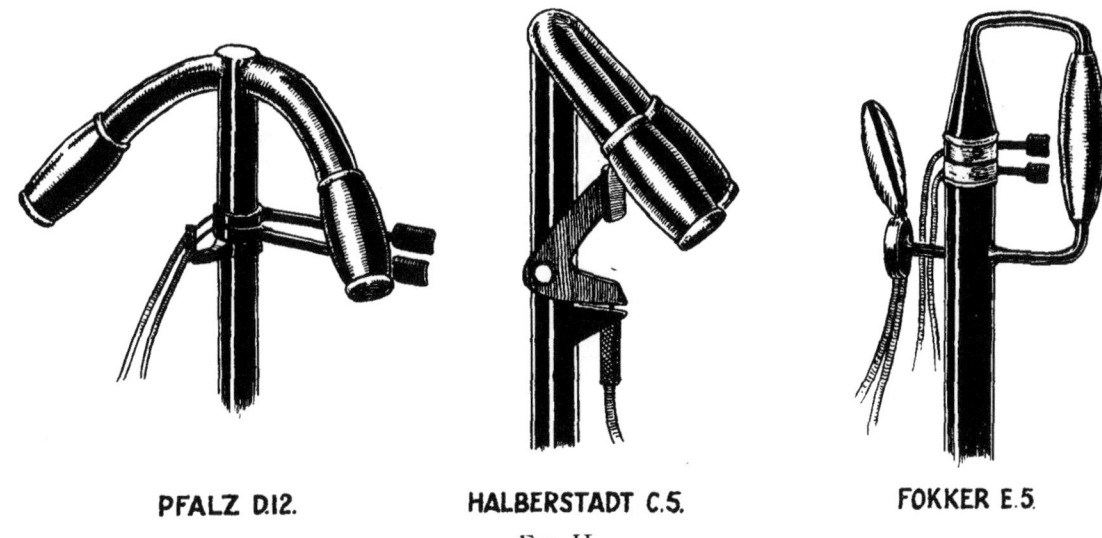

PFALZ D.12.   HALBERSTADT C.5.   FOKKER E.5.

Fig. II.

Halberstadt, Type C. V., 230 Benz, two-seater reconnaissance machine.—The armament of this machine consists of one Spandau synchronised to fire through the propeller for the pilot, and one Parabellum on a rotating ring for the observer.

The mounting for the Spandau gun is not adjustable.

The ammunition box contains about 750 rounds, its special feature being that it has lugs at the mouth of the box to locate the box accurately to the feed block of the gun. No other type of machine was so fitted.

The box is divided off to collect the empty belt on the port side; the gun is fitted on the starboard side of the fuselage and is extremely inaccessible.

The empty belt chute is bolted to the feed block of the gun, and the feed block end of this chute is fitted with a very neat spring back lid, so that the belt can be easily got at in case of a stoppage of the gun.

The gun control is fitted to the top of the control lever of the machine (the control lever top is a T similar to that in the Pfalz). The gun control lever impressed by the thumb, and is pivoted by a bolt passing through the tube forming the control lever itself.

The Parabellum gun is carried on a revolving mounting, the rings being made of wood, and fitted with a special attachment for the gun similar to the one of the L.V.G., a sample of which is being sent over.

Rumpler, C. IV. two-seater reconnaissance machine. 200 H.P. Maybach engine.—The armament of this machine consists of one Spandau for the pilot synchronised to fire through the propeller, and one Parabellum on a rotating ring mounting.

The Spandau gun is as usual in all German machines mounted on the starboard side of the fuselage. The gun mounting is in the form of a cradle bolted to the ply-wood engine bearer. The empty case chute fits up against the discharge port of the gun, and goes through the bottom of the fuselage.

The empty belt is collected in the bottom of the fuselage under the engine, and can be removed by opening a door in the side of the fuselage.

The ammunition box goes right across the fuselage under the engine, and holds about 1,450 rounds of ammunition.

The Parabellum gun is carried on a mounting which very much resembles the Scarff ring mounting. A photograph of this type of mounting was taken on the plate which shows the front of the A.E.G. trench fighter, the only difference being that steel springs are used in place of elastic, and the release for the rotation of the mounting is on the ring itself.

Fokker Biplane, Type D. 7. 180 H.P. Mercedes. Single seater fighter.—The armament of this machine consists of two Spandau guns synchronised to fire through the propeller. These are mounted on a mounting built up from steel tubes in a very neat manner, and the mounting is adjustable; the guns are allowed to swivel on the front support, and are adjustable both laterally and vertically on the rear support.

The vertical adjustment is effected by allowing the tube welded to the rear support fork to slide through a split T piece made by welding two pieces of tube together at right angles to one another. The lateral adjustment is effected by allowing the split horizontal member of this T piece to move sideways along an horizontal member of the fuselage; the adjustment is locked by bolts which clamp the split T piece.

The ammunition box holds 650 rounds for each gun.

The guns are fitted with a round counter similar to the one on the Fokker monoplane (see description above).

The empty belt is collected in a box forward of the ammunition box and the empty cases are thrown overboard through a small chute.

The chute conveying the empty belt to its collecting box has a spring back lid on it near the feed block of the gun, so that access can be easily obtained to the belt.

A gun off one of these machines is coming over for detailed examination.

The guns are operated from the control lever of the machine, the handle on the top of this lever being similar to the one on the Fokker monoplane (see description above.)

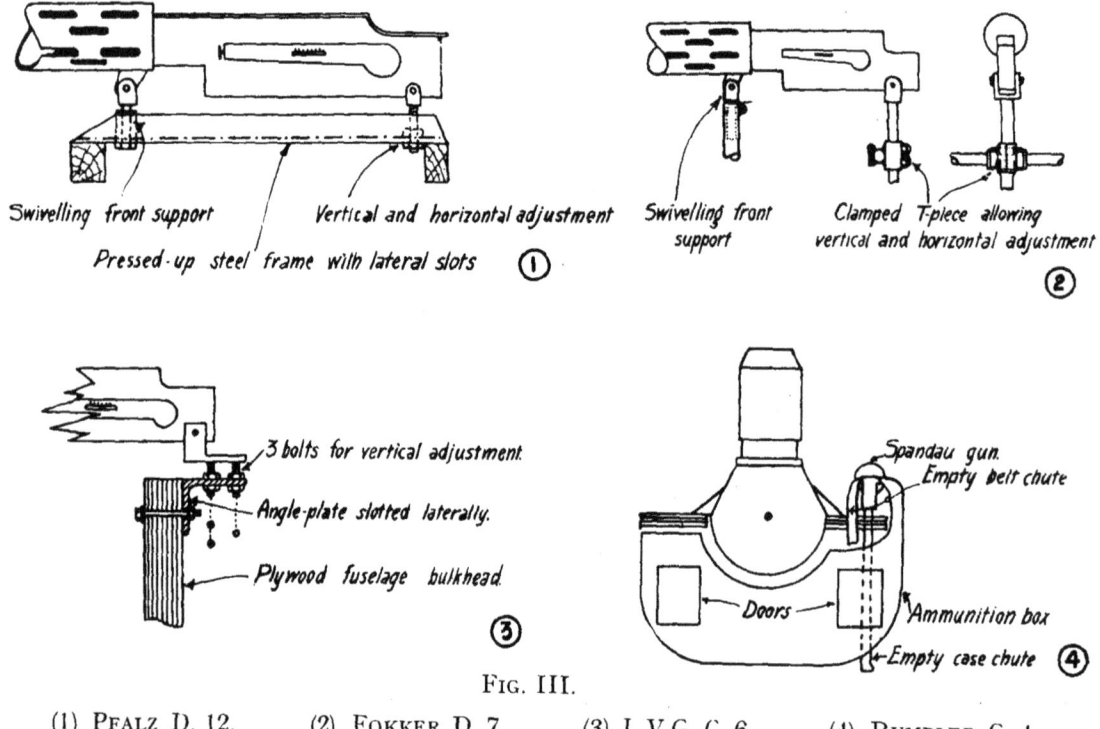

Fig. III.

(1) Pfalz D. 12.   (2) Fokker D. 7.   (3) L.V.G. C. 6.   (4) Rumpler C. 4.

Gotha, two-seater twin engine.—This machine is of interest as it has a fixed Spandau forward firing gun for the pilot, which is not synchronised.

The ammunition box holds 1,000 rounds; the empty cases are thrown overboard, and the empty belt is collected in a box.

The observer has a Parabellum gun, mounted on the usual ring mounting.

A.E.G. 3-seater twin engine, armoured trench fighter.—This machine has two large calibre guns (the guns were not on the machine but the mountings indicate this).

The front observer has a Parabellum mounted on the usual ring mounting and also a heavy gun mounted to fire forward and downward.

Two photos of this were taken, one to show the aspect of the mounting from the outside, the other to show the seat and mounting from the inside of the cockpit.

The rear observer has a Parabellum on a ring mounting and a heavy calibre gun to fire downward through the bottom of the cockpit.

This gun is mounted on a universal joint on the floor.

General Remarks.—In the main the workmanship of all armament is not so good as ours. The German designers do not consider it worth while to introduce anti-friction devices, in the shape of rollers in the ammunition boxes, nor to locate definitely the box to the feed block of the gun. Neither do they consider that the space occupied by the collection of the empty belt is a disadvantage.

The single seater fighters do not carry as many rounds per gun as ours, and the mountings of the guns are not as rigid or simple.

On all the machines seen the synchronising gear is fitted with the usual flexible drive, the gun being brought into action by throwing the gear in or out by a dog clutch, operated by a Bowden wire from the control handle.

The loading handles are all of a very crude and heavy nature, and do not appear to be as easy to manipulate as ours.

I
Front View.

J
Three-quarter Front View of Nacelle and Engine Egg.

K
Three-quarter Rear View.

L
Gun Mounting in Rear Cockpit.

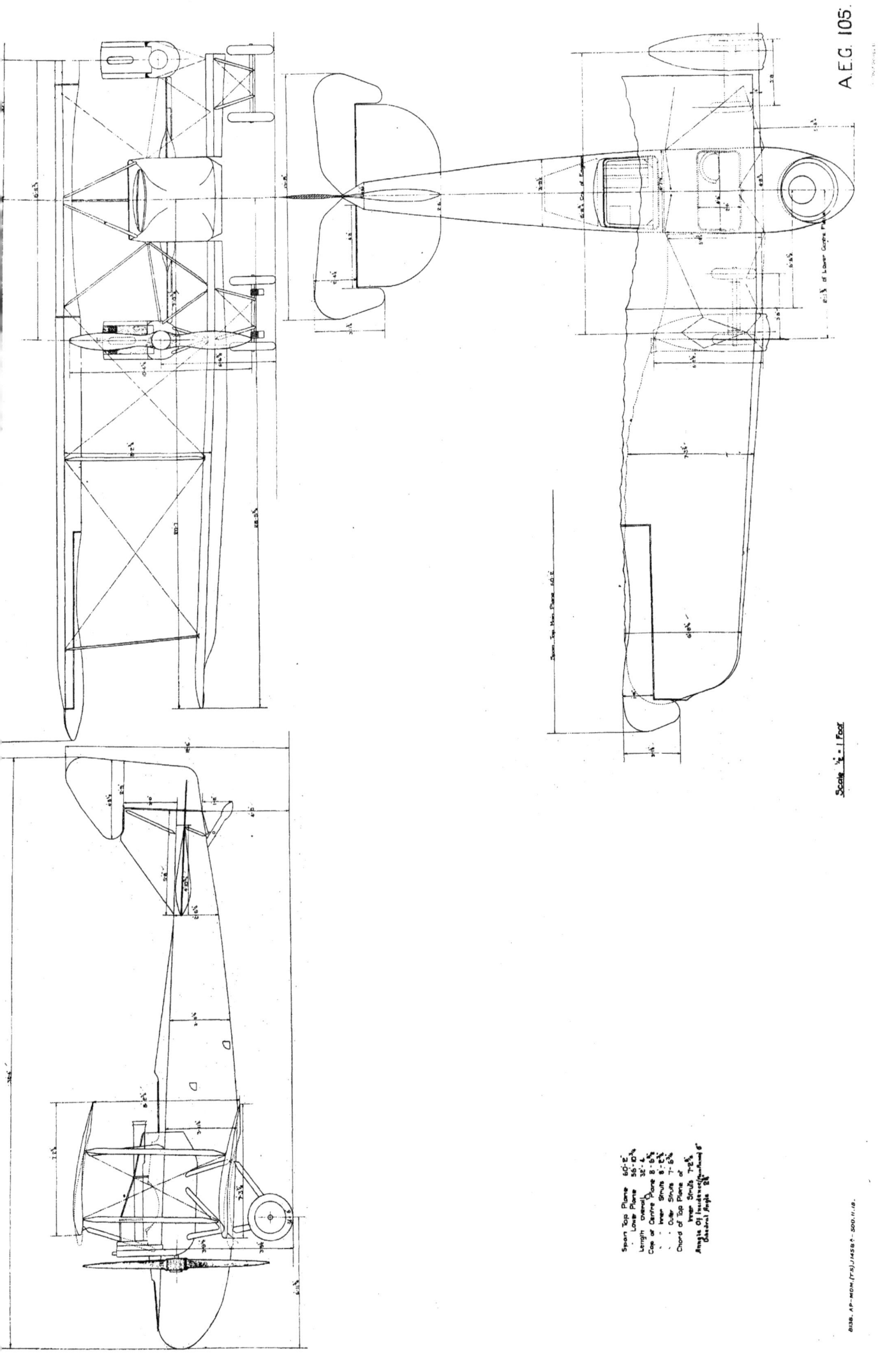

www.ingramcontent.com/pod-product-compliance
Ingram Content Group UK Ltd.
Pitfield, Milton Keynes, MK11 3LW, UK
UKHW051525180426
11947UKWH00019B/1586